PAINTING IN THE DARK
Esref Armagan, Blind Artist

by Rachelle Burk
Illustrated by Claudia Gadotti

TUMBLEHOME | l e a r n i n g, Inc.

For further information, contact:
Tumblehome Learning, Inc.
201 Newbury St, Suite 201
Boston, MA 02116
http://www.tumblehomelearning.com

Library of Congress Control Number: 2016935969

Burk, Rachelle
Painting in the Dark / Rachelle Burk - 1st ed

ISBN 978-1-943431-15-1

Cover Art/Illustration: Claudia Gadotti
Design: Yu-Yi Ling, Barnas Monteith

Printed in Taiwan

10 9 8 7 6 5 4 3 2 1

Dedication

To Beverly Turner, who never says "I can't."

R.B.

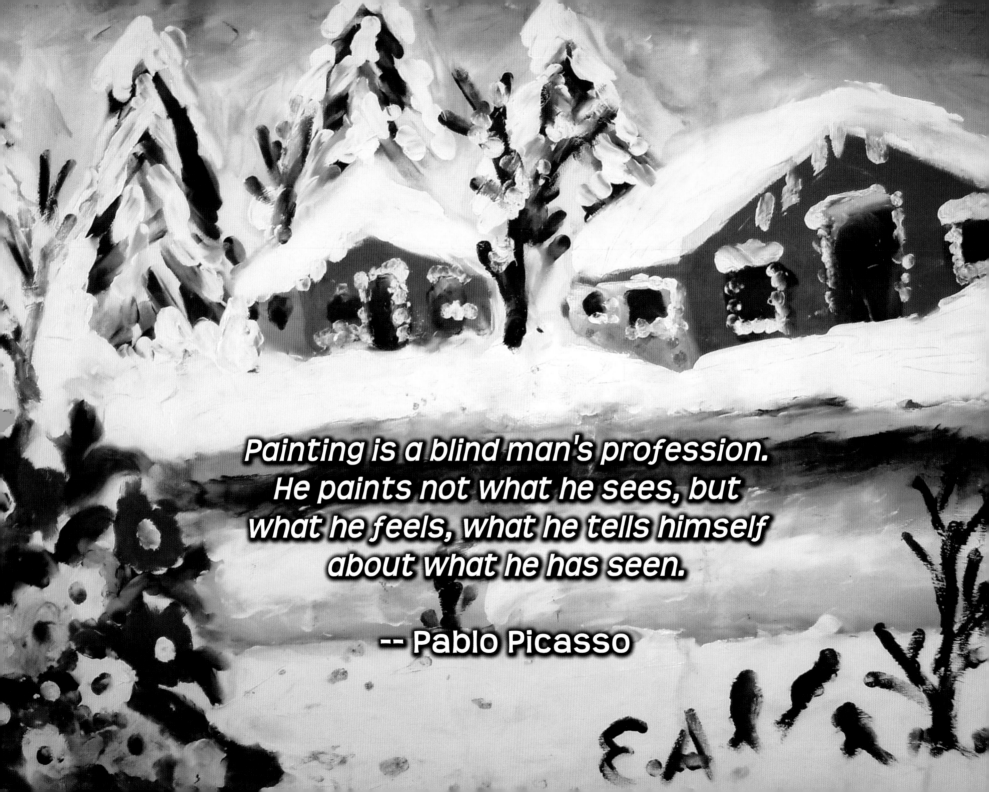

Painting is a blind man's profession. He paints not what he sees, but what he feels, what he tells himself about what he has seen.

-- Pablo Picasso

Esref dabs his finger, sticky with paint, onto a canvas. He adds color and detail until the landscape comes alive. Birds glide before a warm, glowing sunset. A waterfall splashes into a glistening lake. Yet this artist does not know one color from another. His eyes have never gazed upon landscapes like those he paints. He has not even seen his own paintings. That's because Esref has been blind since birth.

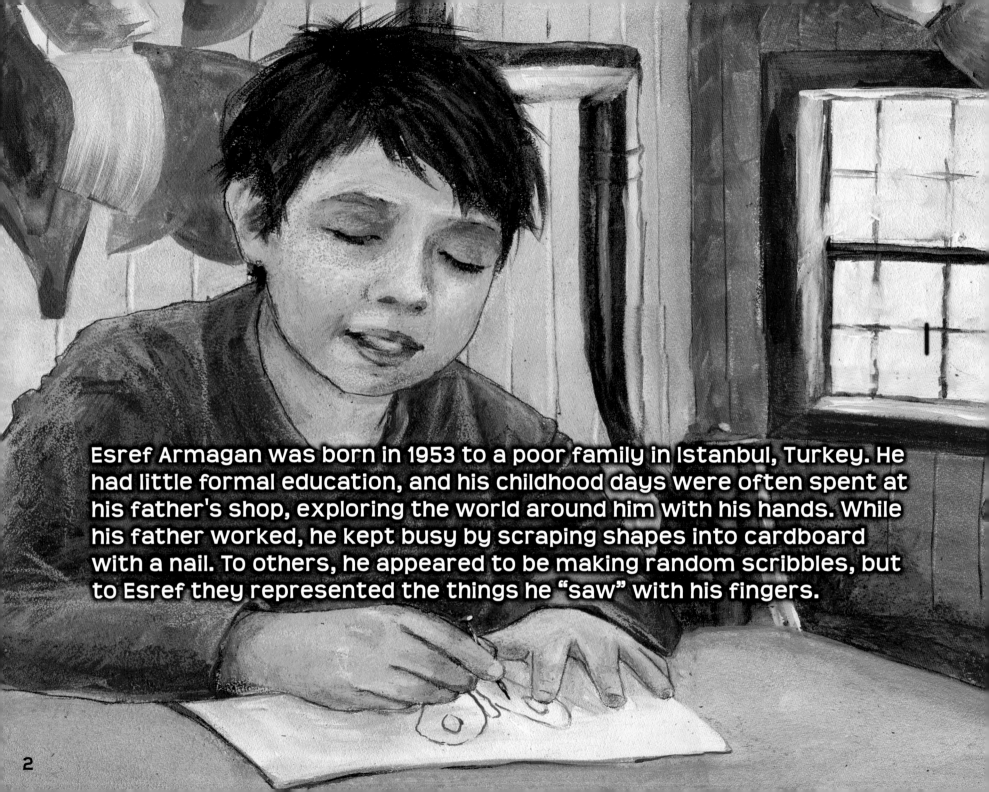

Esref Armagan was born in 1953 to a poor family in Istanbul, Turkey. He had little formal education, and his childhood days were often spent at his father's shop, exploring the world around him with his hands. While his father worked, he kept busy by scraping shapes into cardboard with a nail. To others, he appeared to be making random scribbles, but to Esref they represented the things he "saw" with his fingers.

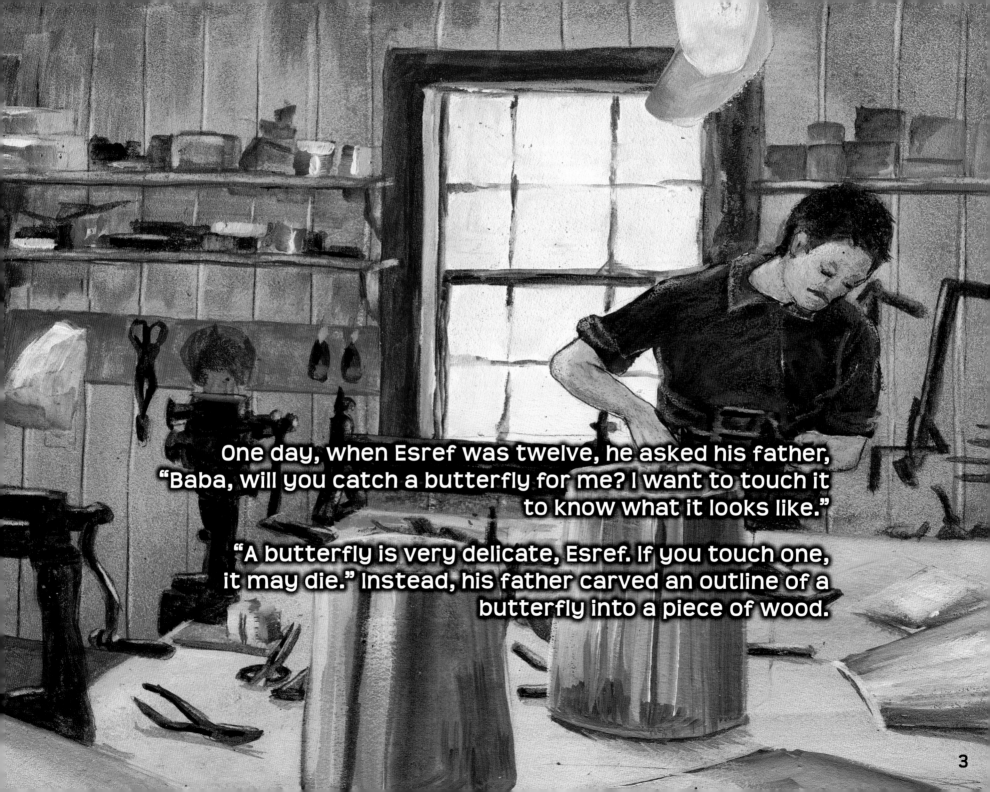

One day, when Esref was twelve, he asked his father, "Baba, will you catch a butterfly for me? I want to touch it to know what it looks like."

"A butterfly is very delicate, Esref. If you touch one, it may die." Instead, his father carved an outline of a butterfly into a piece of wood.

Esref followed the grooves with his fingers. Then, with a nail, he scratched and scraped to reproduce the shape into cardboard. Finally, after many tries, the blind boy drew a butterfly his father was able to recognize.

At the time, however, Esref was not thinking about becoming an artist. He drew to understand his environment, and to feel connected to the world. In this quest, he would face many challenges. While he could understand the shapes of objects by touch, he was curious when he heard people describe things in terms of their colors. What did it mean that the sky is blue, or a shirt is red? He knew only that color was an important characteristic that sighted people used to identify objects.

I will learn to use color so that people can relate to my art, Esref decided when he was fifteen. He asked his father to buy him a set of colored pencils. After drawing a picture onto poster board, Esref filled the image with colors by feeling the borders created by the pencil pressure.

"Baba, please give me a red pencil," he said. His father stopped working to hand Esref the pencil.

"Baba, now I need a yellow one." His father again stopped to help his son.

"Baba, will you…"

His father threw up his hands. "Esref, I cannot work with all your interruptions! I will set the pencils in a row and you can memorize their order." Baba laid them out: white, black, yellow, brown, red, blue, and green.

This was the order that Esref would use from that day forward.

Esref constantly asked about the colors of things. There was a lot to remember: A watermelon skin is green, but the inside is red. The sea appears light blue on a sunny day, and black on a cloudy one. Flowers, butterflies and clothing can be many different colors.

But Esref had a remarkable memory. Once he learned the shapes and colors of objects, he never forgot them, and could draw and paint them on his own.

Esref also overheard people talk about shadows.

One day he proudly showed his father a new picture.

"Look, Baba, I have made a picture of an apple casting its shadow."

"No," Baba laughed, "you have drawn two apples."

Esref had assumed a red apple would cast a red shadow.

His father then explained how shadows worked, and Esref soon learned how to color them correctly.

At eighteen, he began using oil paint. After planning a picture in his head, he painted with his fingers so that he could feel the surface. With oils, it was necessary to wait a day or two for one color to dry before adding another or they would smear. As a result, it often took Esref weeks to complete a single painting.

"Incredible!" people would say when they saw Esref's pictures. "It's almost hard to believe he is blind," some said, peering into his eyes for evidence of sight.

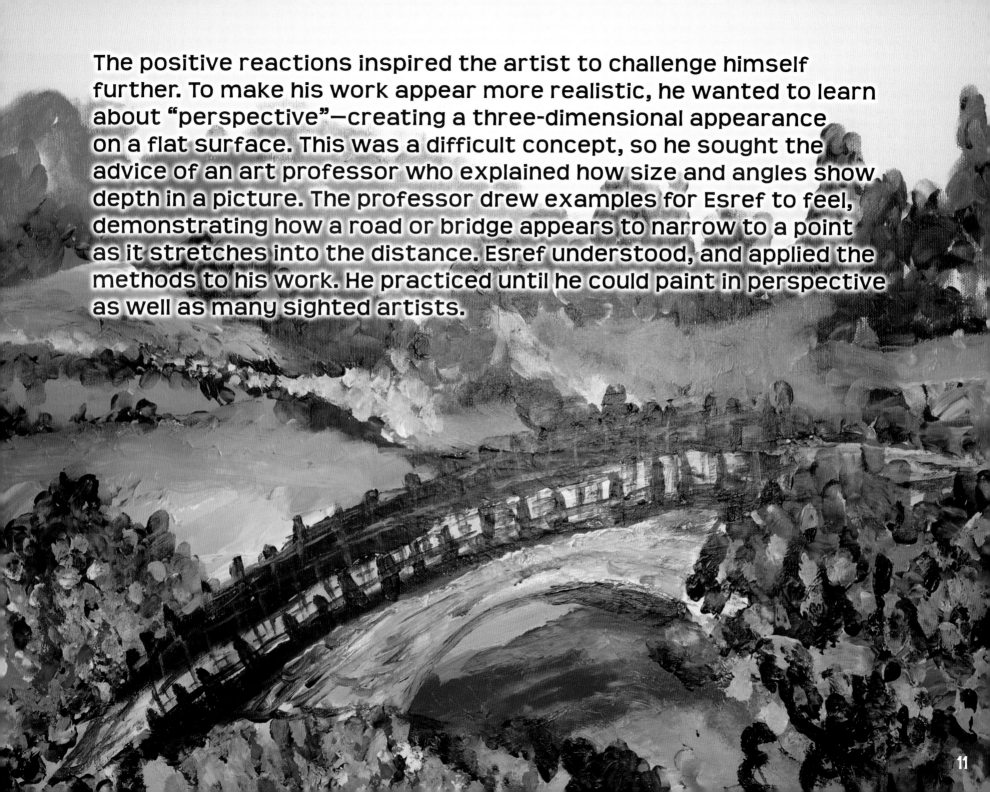

The positive reactions inspired the artist to challenge himself further. To make his work appear more realistic, he wanted to learn about "perspective"—creating a three-dimensional appearance on a flat surface. This was a difficult concept, so he sought the advice of an art professor who explained how size and angles show depth in a picture. The professor drew examples for Esref to feel, demonstrating how a road or bridge appears to narrow to a point as it stretches into the distance. Esref understood, and applied the methods to his work. He practiced until he could paint in perspective as well as many sighted artists.

Eventually Esref got married and fathered two children. As a blind man without an education, however, he struggled to support his family. Sometimes he found odd jobs, but mostly he helped in his father's shop, making and selling tin heating stoves. Despite his struggles, he made time to draw and paint. He wondered if he could make extra money by selling his paintings.

Then in 1988, a member of a civic group called The Lions Club invited Esref to display his art at their monthly meetings. Many of the club members bought his work, and word began to spread about the amazing blind artist. He was featured in local news articles, magazines, and even in a television documentary. Within two years, he went to Holland for his first foreign exhibit.

Esref gained more attention when he began painting portraits of well-known people. After asking someone to trace the details in a photograph, he studied the facial features with his fingers. He reproduced the images onto poster board and added paint.

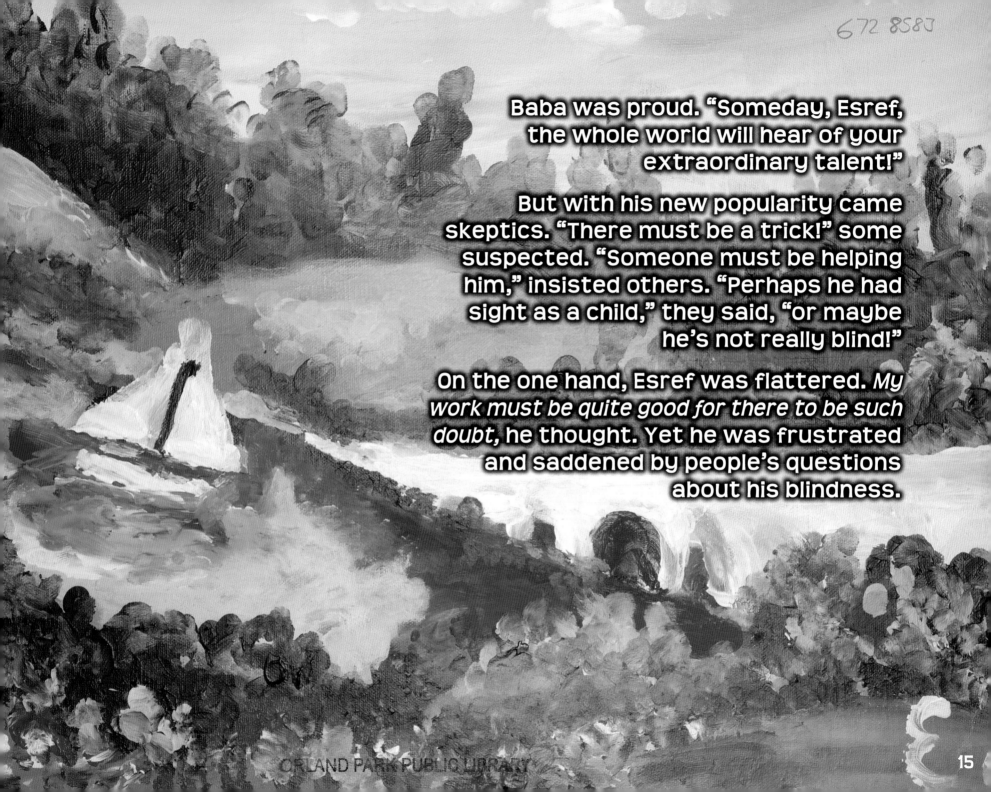

Baba was proud. "Someday, Esref, the whole world will hear of your extraordinary talent!"

But with his new popularity came skeptics. "There must be a trick!" some suspected. "Someone must be helping him," insisted others. "Perhaps he had sight as a child," they said, "or maybe he's not really blind!"

On the one hand, Esref was flattered. *My work must be quite good for there to be such doubt,* he thought. Yet he was frustrated and saddened by people's questions about his blindness.

In 1993, Esref faced the most difficult time in his life. His beloved father and greatest supporter died. Shortly after, his marriage ended. Esref moved into the cramped place that had been his father's shop. With little money to live on, he was poor and often hungry. Esref tried selling parakeets and artificial flowers in the shop, but the businesses failed. Through it all, he continued to paint, using a board placed over his bed to serve as an easel. Occasionally, he'd sell a painting for a few liras, but overall the days left him lonely, and he feared a bleak future.

The following year, an organization for the blind arranged for Esref to exhibit his work in the Czech Republic at a foreign art festival for the visually impaired. Joan Eroncel, an American living in Turkey, was asked to be his guide. Eventually, she became his manager, interpreter, and closest friend. Joan believed in Esref as faithfully as his father had, and was determined that the world should know about him. She promoted his talent by arranging interviews and exhibits around the world.

Over the next few years, Esref
continued to improve his work.

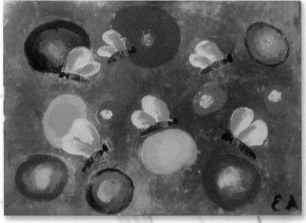

He switched from oil paint to
quick-drying acrylics, and invented
his own artistic techniques.

He hand-crafted stencils, which
enabled him to make identical
images within a picture, such
as multiple windmill blades or
butterfly wings.

The stencils also helped to
prevent the details in the pictures
from smearing.

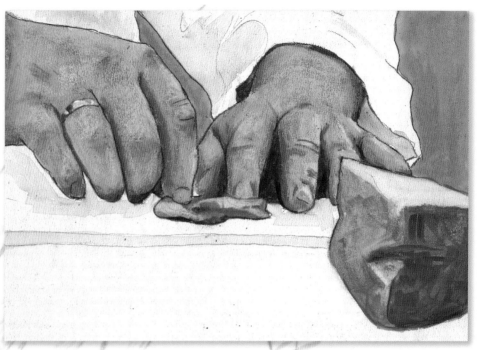

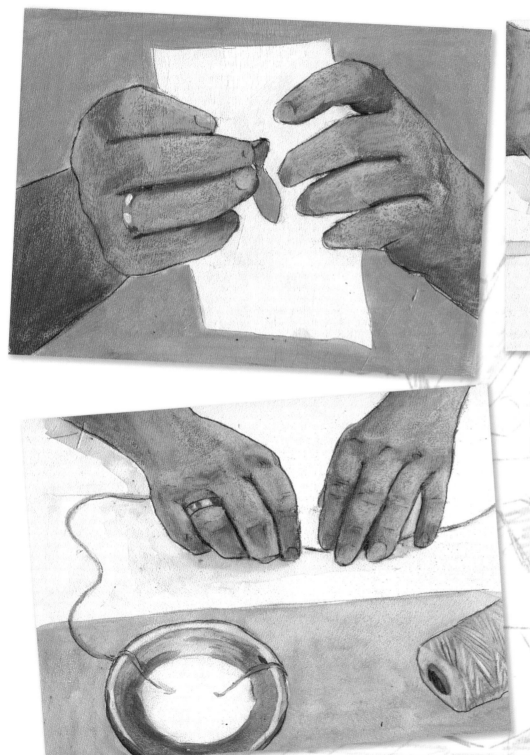

The innovative artist also developed a special type of "relief" painting. By molding bits of clay onto his canvas, he could raise and shape images before painting them. Schools of fish and performing clowns seemed to leap from the pictures! A few years later, he invented yet another technique. By dipping thick thread into craft glue, he could shape details onto the canvas. When it dried, he could paint neatly within the textured borders.

19

While more people noticed Esref's work, he was frustrated by the many who questioned whether he was truly blind and painted without assistance. In 2004, however, scientists gave him the opportunity to put his unusual abilities to the test. Esref was invited to the United States where he met with a team of researchers. There, an eye doctor examined Esref and found that one eye had never formed, and the other was diseased. Using special medical equipment, the doctor tested the reaction of Esref's eyes and brain to stimulation such as flashing lights. The tests confirmed that Esref was completely blind, and likely had been since birth.

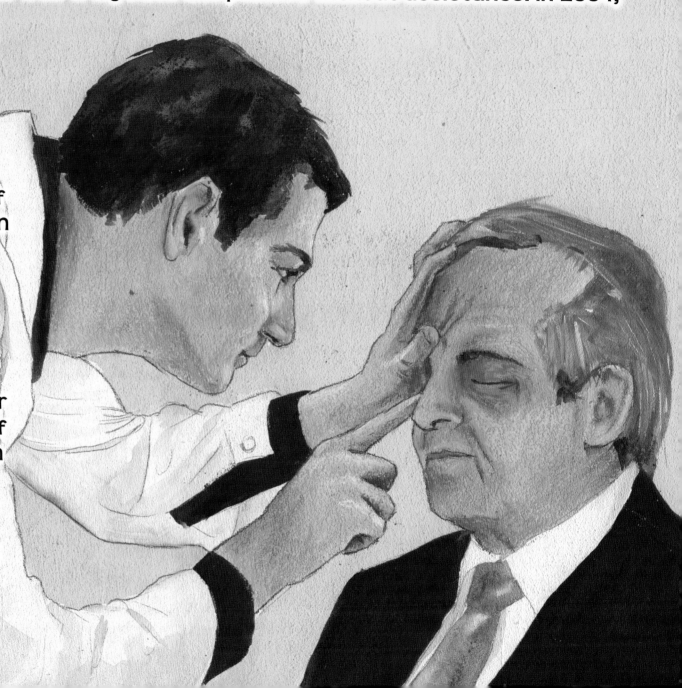

Then Esref met with Dr. John M. Kennedy, a psychologist and expert on artistic development in the blind. Kennedy challenged Esref with increasingly difficult tasks: *Draw a road leading away, with cars at different distances. Feel these objects and draw them from above, from the sides, and at various angles. Draw wheels in motion.*

Although these challenges would be difficult even for a sighted person, Esref tackled them with confidence and succeeded at every one. The researchers were stunned by his abilities. "He took my breath away," said Kennedy. "This man is astounding!" Esref was the first known blind-from-birth person to have mastered perspective.

But how could a person who had never known sight draw objects as if he could see? To understand how Esref's brain worked, doctors put him inside a machine that uses a scanning technology called fMRI (functional magnetic resonance imaging). It recorded the activity in various parts of his brain. While he drew pictures, the part of his brain associated with sight became active—a finding that surprised the scientists. This indicated that, without vision, the brain can "rewire" itself, allowing fingertips to provide the same information to the brain as the eyes do.

This historical discovery was a breakthrough in the understanding of the brain and our senses. The research could even help scientists develop new technologies that would aid blind people in "seeing" through other senses.

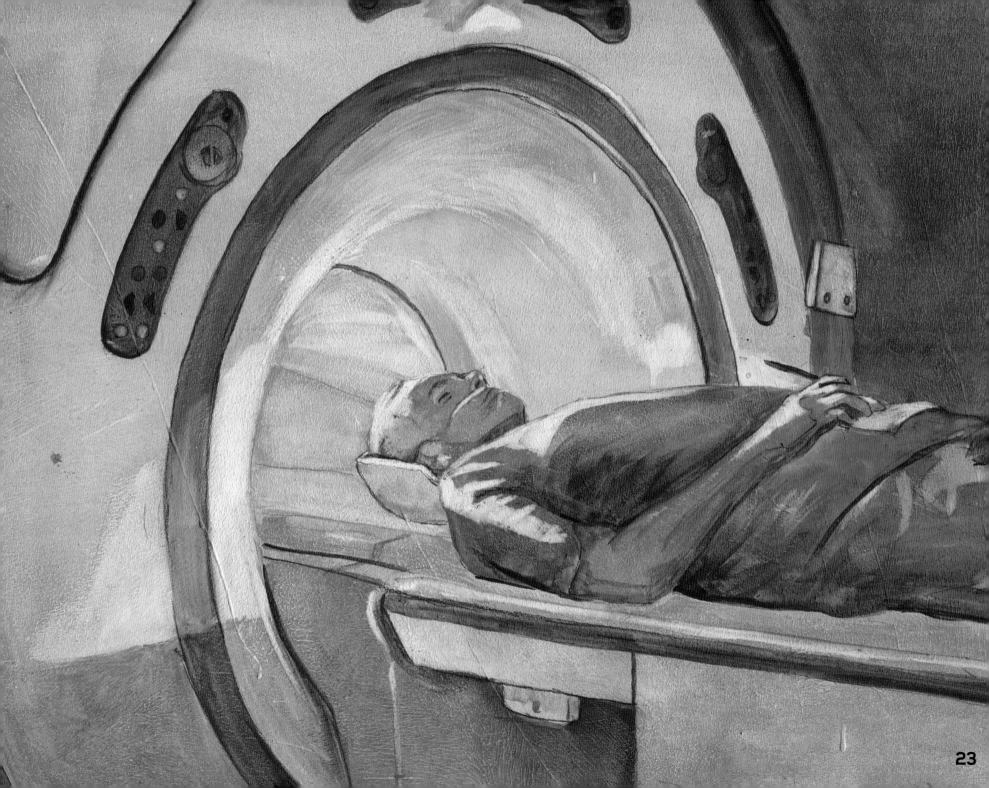

Esref returned to Turkey, finally having proof that he was not a fake.

But while the scientific community was now aware of Esref's incredible talent, he remained largely unknown to the rest of the world. He and his new wife Nilufer, a blind poet, lived on little income.

To make matters worse, his health was failing. His whole body ached, and he was having difficulty walking, but doctors did not know what was wrong. As his illness progressed, he worried that it would affect his ability to paint. Esref felt hopeless and depressed. He questioned whether he would ever realize his dream of being seen as a serious artist.

Meanwhile, a major television company became interested in Esref after reading the scientific reports of his abilities. When they featured him in a documentary about "real superhumans," millions of television viewers worldwide watched his dancing fingers bring to life a shimmering sea of rolling waves, soaring seagulls, and distant sailing boats.

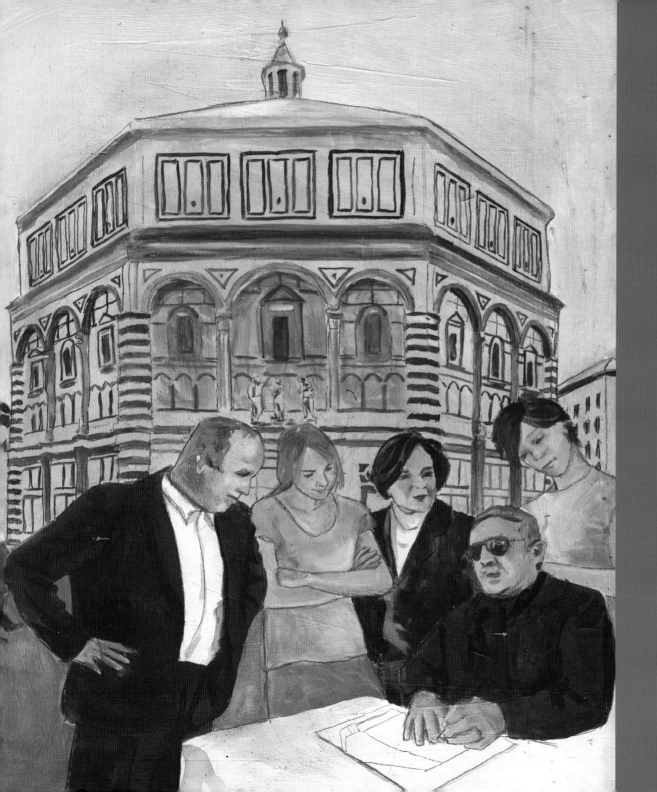

Before the cameras, Esref drew a famous eight-sided building in Italy, making history as the only blind person to ever draw in three-point perspective. Esref had proved that you don't need eyes to see.

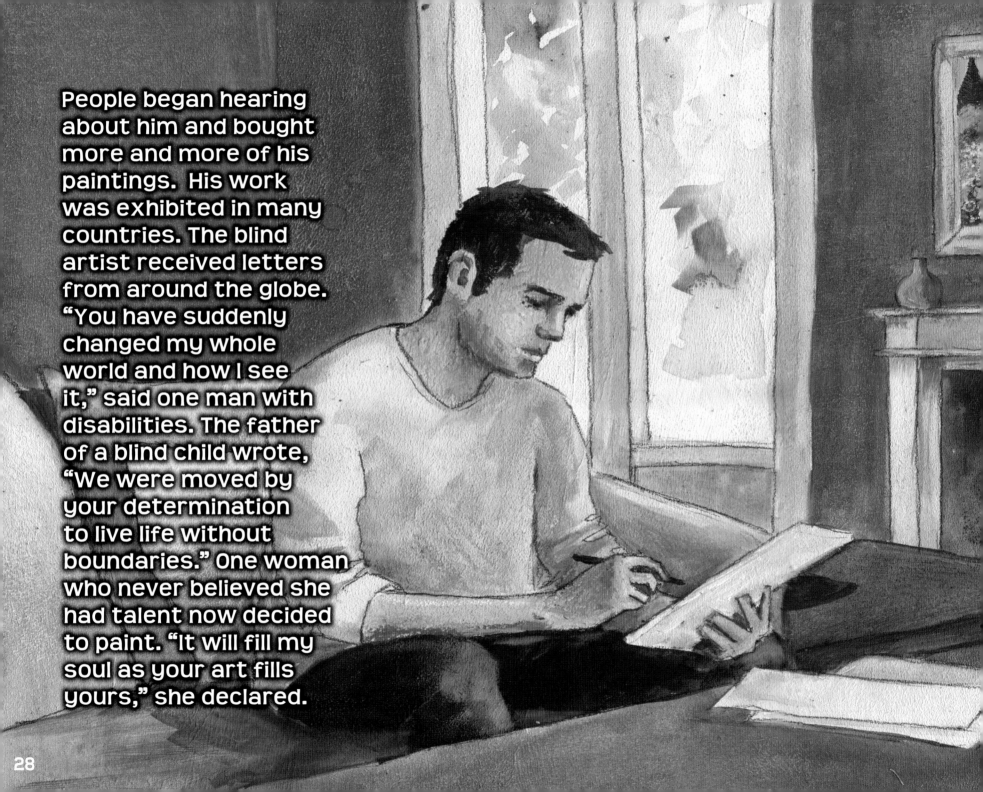

People began hearing about him and bought more and more of his paintings. His work was exhibited in many countries. The blind artist received letters from around the globe. "You have suddenly changed my whole world and how I see it," said one man with disabilities. The father of a blind child wrote, "We were moved by your determination to live life without boundaries." One woman who never believed she had talent now decided to paint. "It will fill my soul as your art fills yours," she declared.

Esref was pleased to have inspired so many people. "By working in a visual area as a blind person," he said, "I have shown that there are no obstacles that can't be overcome."

Having finally achieved his lifelong dream, Esref knew that his father's words had become a reality: *Someday, Esref, the whole world will hear of your extraordinary talent!*

Author's Note

I first discovered Esref Armagan (pronounced Esh-ref Ar-mon) after stumbling upon an online article about him. Captivated, I wanted to know how a person born totally blind could paint images of things he had never seen. Furthermore, why would he *want* to create art that he himself would never see? From that moment, I resolved to learn everything I could about this remarkable man. What followed were Skype interviews with Armagan (interpreted by Joan Eroncel), emails with the scientists who researched his brain and abilities, chats with art instructors on the concept of perspective drawing, and countless hours studying videos and paintings. I set out to write a book that would bring Armagan's inspiring story to more people, especially those with disabilities and their loved ones.

The fact that Armagan is completely self-taught speaks much about his creativity. He learned about color, shadow, and reflection by endlessly asking sighted people to describe such things, then practicing until they told him he had it right.

Evident in many of Armagan's paintings his use of *linear perspective.* This is a geometric method of representing on paper the way that objects further away appear smaller and closer together. He has also demonstrated his ability to paint in two- and three- point perspective, showing objects as they would be viewed from various corners, as well as from above or below.

The artist's talent was first discovered by an Istanbul chapter of the Lions Club, an international civic organization with a commitment to aiding the blind and visually impaired. Today there are Lions chapters in over 200 countries.

Armagan contributed to scientific studies of human perception when he agreed to have his brain scanned through *fMRI.* Functional magnetic resonance imaging is a technique for measuring brain responses. It uses a powerful electro-magnetic scanner that looks at changes in oxygen and blood flow in various parts of the brain to detect areas of activity. Measuring these changes, which are captured on a computer, helps scientists understand more about how the brain works.

In 2008, doctors diagnosed Armagan's mysterious ailment as *ankylosing spondylitis,* a painful and progressive form of arthritis. Despite his illness, he continues to paint, refusing to let any obstacle hinder his dream.

Resources, Source Notes, and Further Reading

ORGANIZATIONS

Art Beyond Sight is a non-profit organization whose mission is to promote equal access to art experiences for all people. Through their program **Art Education for the Blind (AEB)** they have created ways for people without sight to learn about and create art. Visit: *www.ArtBeyondSight.org*. Esref demonstrates how he paints, including his use of hand-made stencils, in a video produced by ABS: *http://www.artbeyondsight.org/sidebar/aboutus.shtml*

BOOKS

Art History Through Touch and Sound. *Available in blind-accessible format.* A history of art from prehistoric to contemporary, with over 600 images with verbal descriptions, printable tactile diagrams with guidance of hands, interpretive sound compositions, art activities and teaching tips. *Free online through AEB:* *http://www.artbeyondsight.org/ahtts/index.shtml*

*Jackson, Donna. **Phenomena: Secrets of the Senses**. New York: Little, Brown Books for Young Readers, 2008. *Artistic Touch* (pp. 97-107). (*This book is for young readers)*

Hayhoe, Simon. **Arts, Culture, and Blindness: A Study of Blind Students in the Visual Arts.** Youngstown, NY: Teneo, 2008.

NEWSPAPER AND MAGAZINE

Motluk, Alison. "**The Art of Seeing Without Sight**," *New Scientist,* January 29, 2005.

Feinberg, Cara. "**Old Brain, New Tricks**," *The Boston Globe*, January 15, 2005.

RESEARCH ARTICLES

Perception Studies by Dr. John M. Kennedy:

Kennedy, J.M. and Juricevic, I. Foreshortening, convergence and drawings from a blind adult. *Perception* 2006: 35, 847–851. Blind man draws using convergence in three dimensions. *Psychonomic Bulletin and Review* 2006, 13 (3), 506-509.

fMRI study:

Amedi A, Merabet LB , Camprodon J, Bermpohl F, Fox S, Ronen I, Kim D and Pascual-Leone A. Neural and behavioral correlates of drawing in an early blind painter: A case study. *Brain Research* 2008; 1242: 252-262.

VIDEOS/TV

Discovery Channel. "The Real Superhumans," Television documentary, 2008. (See YouTube)

FOR MORE INFORMATION

Links to articles, videos, interviews, and organizations for the visually impaired, visit: *www.EsrefArmagan.blogspot.com*

About the Author and Illustrator

Rachelle Burk is a children's author of both fiction and nonfiction. She is also a social worker, storyteller, and rescue squad volunteer. Rachelle lives in New Jersey with her fabulous husband, Fred, with whom she loves to travel, scuba dive, hike, and explore caves. Other books by the author include *The Walking Fish, Tree House in a Storm, Don't Turn the Page!, The Tooth Fairy Trap, Miss Crump's Funny Bone,* and *Sleep Soundly at Beaver's Inn.*

Artist **Claudia Gadotti** is an illustrator and portrait painter with more than a decade of experience. She graduated from the Academy of Art University with a BFA and a major in illustration, presently working mostly with children's books, book covers, magazines, and portraits. Claudia grew up in Italy and currently lives and works in New Zealand.

Acknowledgements

The author expresses her gratitude to the many people who provided content suggestions for this book. In particular, she thanks psychologist Dr. John M. Kennedy for his expert technical explanations and invaluable help, and Joan Eroncel for her advice, her translation help, and her deep understanding of Esref's history, health, struggles and techniques. Neuroscientist Amir Amedi formed part of Esref's brain scan team and helped explain the findings. Lion Mahesh Chitnis, past governor of Lions Clubs International in New Jersey was instrumental in providing funding for for a braille version of this book.

Photo & Art Credits

The paintings in the illustrations are actual embedded photos of Esref's artwork. We would like to acknowledge and thank Joan Eroncel for coordinating the licensing of Esref's various works for this book. The perspective sketches on page 21 and the watermarked Baptistery sketch on page 26, are also actual drawings by Esref Armagan, used with the permission of Dr. John M. Kennedy (the psychologist referenced on page 21). Barbara Oswald, owner of Seattle's Mt. Baker Neighborhood Center for the Arts, generously donated several images of Armagan's artwork. Turkish photographer Zafer Kizilkaya donated painting images as well as the photo of Esref Armagan on Author's Note page.